I Want to Be a Lawyer

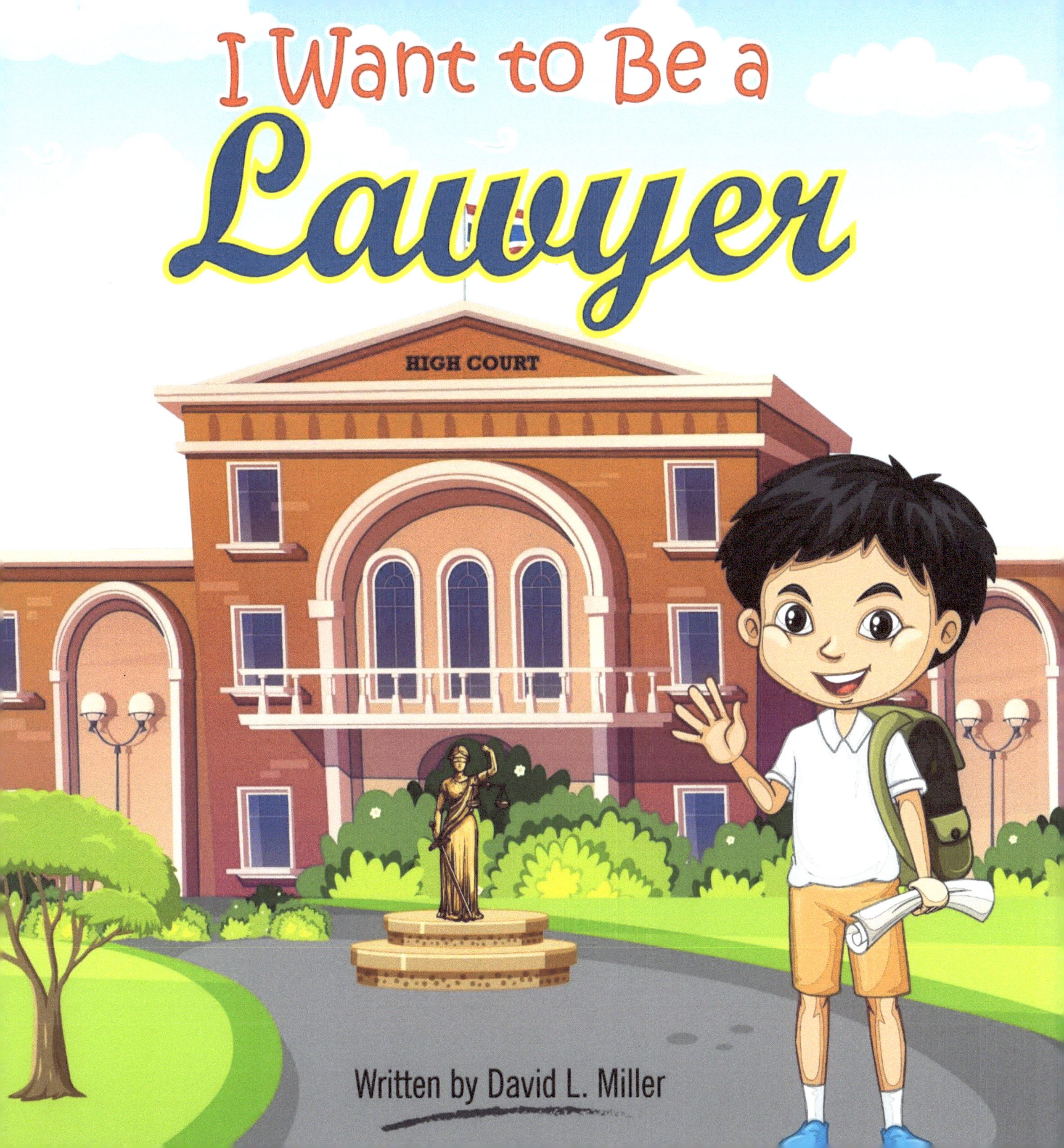

Written by David L. Miller

Liam wanted to be something new.
But first, there was a few things he would have to do.

Liam imagined standing up in court.
But he would need a stool because he's so short.

Liam imagined staying organized with all the papers. He wanted to help his friends, family, and neighbors.

Liam imagined sitting at the table and writing with his pen.
And he would like to say objection again and again.

Liam imagined reading a book with glasses on his face.
And he imagined talking to the judge to make his case.

Liam wants to be a lawyer but he's still so small.
But he knows one day he'll be a lawyer standing tall.

"I want to be a lawyer," Liam would say.
He knows that it will take work to be a lawyer someday.

iam grabs a journal and writes out his list.
le writes so much he feels a kink in his wrist.

But Liam knows what he wants to be.
He'll do whatever it takes to be a lawyer you see.

He'll have to finish high school and then off to college.
He'll need to study and gain all of the knowledge.

He'll have to follow the laws too and avoid any trouble.
And then he'll study some more even when it's a struggle.

ometimes Liam may feel a little stressed.
specially when he has to pass the LSAT test.

Then there will be a bit more school Liam has to get through. And over time Liam just grew and grew.

iam works hard and goes to class.
hen there is one last exam he has to pass.

Then Liam's dream is complete, he is finally fulfilled.
He's a lawyer now and so very skilled.

Liam can follow his dream and always fight.
And as a lawyer, he can do what is right.

“I want to be a lawyer," Liam used to say.
And now he is a lawyer each and every day.

About The Author

The author David L. Miller has written many books on a variety of topics. “Rules for the Single Dude” (Men’s Health Advice Book); the joke book series “Comic on the Corner", and the Children’s Books “I WANT TO BE A LAWYER" and "KINDNESS GOES A LONG WAY."

www.ingramcontent.com/pod-product-compliance
Ingram Content Group UK Ltd.
Pitfield, Milton Keynes, MK11 3LW, UK
UKHW061030310726
14089UKWH00009B/181
* 9 7 8 9 6 9 2 3 9 2 0 0 6 *